AUTHENTIC JAZZ PLAYALONG

It Don't Mean A Thing

10 JAZZ STANDARDS FOR FLUTE

Edited by Andy Hampton

© 2006 by Faber Music Ltd
First published in 2006 by Faber Music Ltd
Music processed by MusicSet 2000
Design by Kenosha
Printed in England by Caligraving Ltd

ISBN10 0-571-52738-8
EAN13 978-0-571-52738-0

Music arranged and recorded by Artemis Music Ltd
Introductory text by Chris Ingham
℗ 2006 by Faber Music Ltd © 2006 by Faber Music Ltd

Drums: Matt Skelton
Bass: Jeremy Bro
Piano: James Pearson

To buy Faber Music publications or to find out about the
full range of titles available please contact your
local retailer or Faber Music sales enquiries:

Faber Music Limited, Burnt Mill, Elizabeth Way, Harlow CM20 2HX England
Tel: +44 (0) 1279 82 89 82 Fax: +44 (0) 1279 82 89 83
sales@fabermusic.com
fabermusic.com

CONTENTS

TRACK LIST

HOW TO USE THIS BOOK

This book contains 10 classic jazz tunes, each of which is an essential part of the core jazz repertoire.

LEARNING THE SONGS

There are many approaches to improvising on standards, but they all have one thing in common: they follow the form of the song. Some players (the great Louis Armstrong being the most notable) base their improvisations on the melody, and the tune never seems far away in their solos. Others (too many to mention, but Charlie Parker is a good example) get right inside the complexities of the harmonies, so that their solos seem to outline, reinforce and explore the harmonic movement of a chord sequence.

It can be useful to learn some theory (e.g. which notes to play over a given chord in a certain context) but all good jazz musicians combine theory with melodic fragments, rhythmic feel and gut instinct to make their statement. One thing is certain – it's hard to play good jazz without a strong sense of rhythm. So groove, feel and style are as important as which notes you choose to play.

Each song falls into two main sections:

THE 'HEAD'

Each song starts with a statement of the original melody of the song (original lyrics are given for reference), which is known as the 'head'.

IMPROVISATION SECTION

The second half of the piece gives you a chance to hone your improvisational skills. In the score you will find a selection of ideas or starting points for improvisation, which are notated in cue size. These phrases are not compulsory – rather they are there to provide inspiration for your own ideas. You may find it easier to start by using the sample phrases before you go on to develop other melodic ideas of your own.

A BRIEF GUIDE TO THE SONGS

IT DON'T MEAN A THING (IF IT AIN'T GOT THAT SWING)
(Ellington-Mills)

Following a period of playing for sit-down audiences in theatres in 1931, Duke Ellington's manager Irving Mills noticed that Ellington and his orchestra — by now playing for dancers in a Chicago café — had lost a little of their bounce. 'The people were not dancing properly', Mills remembered, 'the tempo wasn't there'. He mentioned it to Duke, advising him that the music 'don't mean a thing if it ain't got that swing'. Amused, Duke immediately began writing a tune around Mills's spontaneous phrase and a classic was born. First recorded in 1932 with Ivie Anderson on vocals, it has been covered countless times since, from swing-oriented players (Lionel Hampton, Stephane Grapelli), modernists (Thelonious Monk, Stan Getz) and contemporary musicians (Lynne Arriale, Benny Green).

BLUES IN THE NIGHT
(Arlen-Mercer)

'Blues in the night' is a meditation on the blues reflecting both composer Harold Arlen's and lyricist Johnny Mercer's sophistication and shared love of jazz. It originates from the writers' first collaboration on 1941 movie *Blues in the night*, a portrait of big-band life, and was a big hit. Its famous opening line — 'My momma done tol' me', which Arlen had to retrieve from pages of Mercer's lyric ideas — became a fashionable catchphrase. It has been covered by many singers (including Mercer and Arlen themselves) and bands (notably Jimmy Lunceford and Woody Herman) though a good place to hear the dramatic possibilities of the piece is the Frank Sinatra-Nelson Riddle version on *Only the lonely* (1958).

MY FUNNY VALENTINE
(Rodgers-Hart)

Written for the 1938 Rodgers/Hart musical *Babes in arms*, this tune become such a cabaret standard, one jaded East Side New York nightclub owner inserted a clause into his singers' contracts forbidding them to perform it! It is a love song full of insults, with references of a figure 'less than Greek' and a mouth 'a little weak', but most vocalists approach it simply as a classic, quirky love song, while instrumentalists continue to be drawn to its musical beauty.

EMBRACEABLE YOU
(Gershwin-Gershwin)

Written in 1930 by Gershwin brothers George (composer) and Ira (lyricist) for their Broadway show *Girl Crazy*, it was sung in the original show by Ginger Rogers and Allen Kearns while the 1943 film version of the show featured Judy Garland's interpretation. One of the most famous jazz versions is Charlie Parker's 1947 recording; an improvisation on the chords making very little reference to Gershwin's original melody at all!

LOVE IS HERE TO STAY
(Gershwin-Gershwin)

The final song the Gershwin brothers wrote together before composer George died of a brain tumour in 1937, 'Love is here to stay' appeared originally in the 1938 movie *Goldwyn Follies*. Sung by Kenny Baker in the film, it has since been among the most covered of Gershwin's songs, a favourite of singers and instrumentalists alike. Tenor saxophonist Ben Webster always brought a tough romanticism to his several recordings of it while Ella Fitzgerald's lushly arranged George Gershwin Songbook version is a classic.

I'VE GOT YOU UNDER MY SKIN
(Porter)

Sung originally as a leisurely beguine by Virginia Bruce to James Stewart in the 1936 movie *Born to dance*, following the famous Frank Sinatra-Nelson Riddle treatment of 1956, 'I've got you under my skin' is commonly played as a swing tune. It is a dramatic 56-bar Cole Porter song, so the easiest way of navigating the material is to learn the song itself, as if you had to sing it.

HOW HIGH THE MOON
(Hamilton-Lewis)

The only enduring 'standard' from the writing team of composer Morgan Lewis and lyricist Nancy Hamilton, 'How high the moon' was originally sung as a wistful ballad by Alfred Drake in the 1940 Broadway revue *Two for the show*. Since then it has been adopted as an up-tempo vehicle for improvisers, largely due to its popularity as a 'bop anthem' during the mid 1940s. Sometimes the tune was credited, as in Don Byas's 1944 recording, other times the chord sequence was borrowed and a new tune composed, as in Bennie Harris's 'Ornithology' (based on the opening phrase of a Charlie Parker solo recorded with Jay McShann in 1942), recorded by Charlie Parker in 1946.

I GET A KICK OUT OF YOU
(Porter)

Part of Cole Porter's 1934 Broadway show *Anything Goes* (which also spawned enduring standards 'You're the top' and 'Anything Goes'), 'I get a kick out of you' has been recorded many times, especially by singers (from Ethel Merman to Mark Murphy to Jamie Cullum) though probably remains most associated with Frank Sinatra after his 1954 version on Songs for young lovers and many vivid concert performances. It has also been tackled by a handful of jazz artists, including Errol Garner, Bud Powell, Clifford Brown and Charlie Parker.

SUMMERTIME
(Gershwin-Gershwin-Heyward-Heyward)

George Gershwin was looking for suitable material to develop into an opera when he came across the novel *Porgy* and he invited the author Du Bose Heyward to collaborate on the libretto. One of Heyward's lyrics that Gershwin struggled to set was the lullaby 'Summertime', which went through several rewrites before the familiar song was born. *Porgy and Bess* premiered in Boston in October 1935 and 'Summertime' was the opening number. Originally sung in the soprano register, it soon became as much part of the jazz and classic pop repertoire as the operatic, with hundreds of interpretations by all manner of musicians. A classic jazz-influenced vocal version is on Ella Fitzgerald and Louis Armstrong's 1957 *Porgy and Bess* album and a classic jazz instrumental performance is on Miles Davis's 1958 collaboration with Gil Evans, *Porgy and Bess*.

SOMEONE TO WATCH OVER ME
(Gershwin-Gershwin)

Composed for the Gershwin brothers' 1924 hit Broadway show *Oh, Kay!*, composer George originally conceived it as a rhythmic piece with a bright tempo and even produced a piano roll with him playing it as such. However, when he played it to lyricist brother Ira at a slower pace, both men realised the piece was a 'wistful and warm one' and Ira fashioned an appropriately longing lyric. It was sung in the show by Gertrude Lawrence to a rag doll and has since been recorded hundreds of times by singers (from Sinatra to Sting) and instrumentalists (from Coleman Hawkins to Brad Mehldau).

CD TRACK 11

BLUES IN THE NIGHT

Words by Johnny Mercer
Music by Harold Arlen

Improvisation

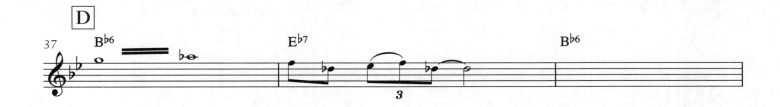

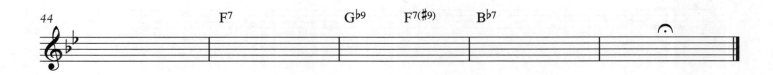

EMBRACEABLE YOU

Music and Lyrics by
George Gershwin and Ira Gershwin

Warner/Chappell Music Ltd, London W6 8BS

Improvisation

IT DON'T MEAN A THING (IF IT AIN'T GOT THAT SWING)

Words by Irving Mills
Music by Duke Ellington

Improvisation

MY FUNNY VALENTINE

Words by Lorenz Hart
Music by Richard Rodgers

Improvisation

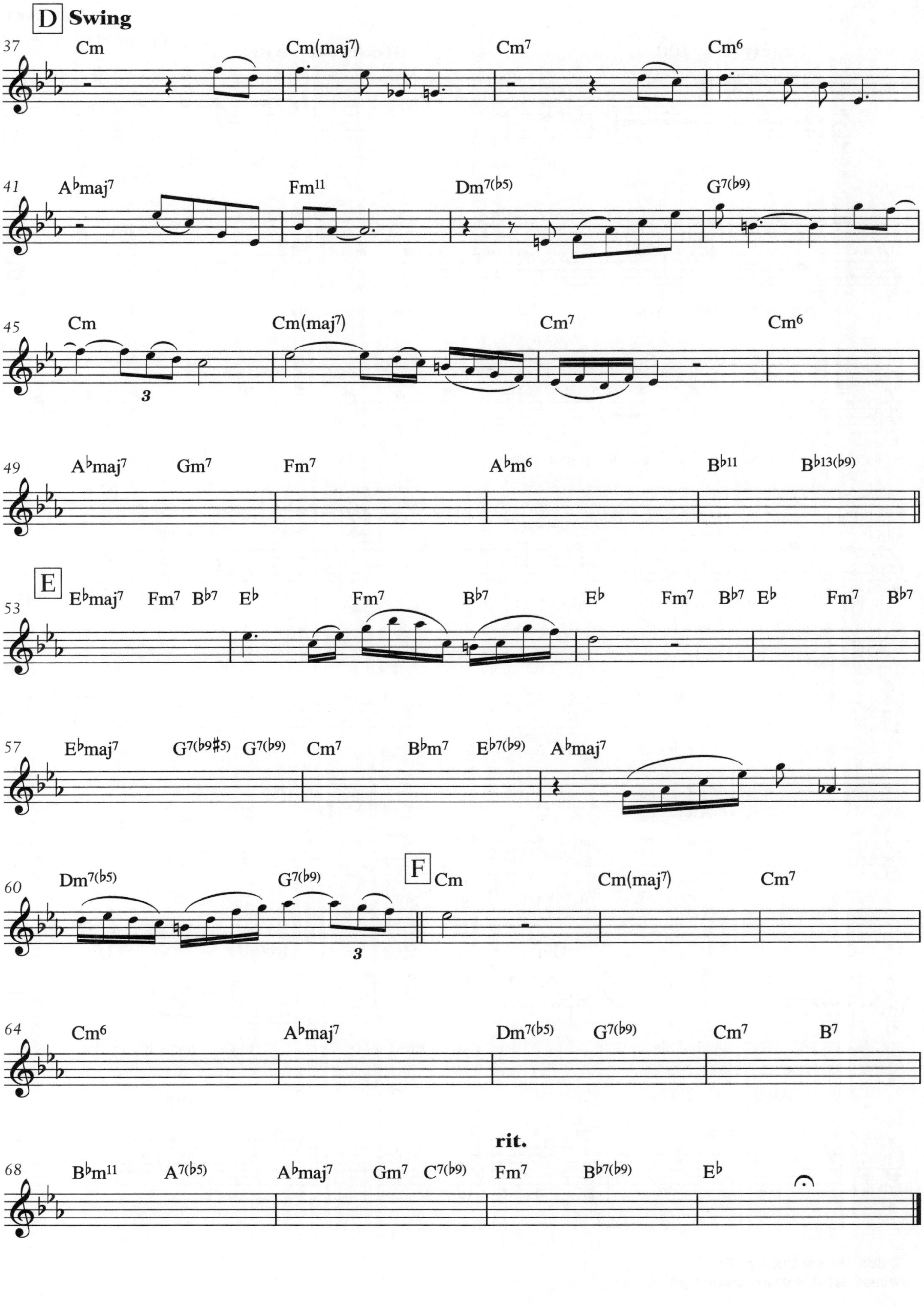

LOVE IS HERE TO STAY

Music and Lyrics by
George Gershwin and Ira Gershwin

Improvisation

C

D

SUMMERTIME

(from *Porgy and Bess*®)

Music and Lyrics by George Gershwin,
Du Bose and Dorothy Heyward and Ira Gershwin

Improvisation

SOMEONE TO WATCH OVER ME

Music and Lyrics by
George Gershwin and Ira Gershwin

Improvisation

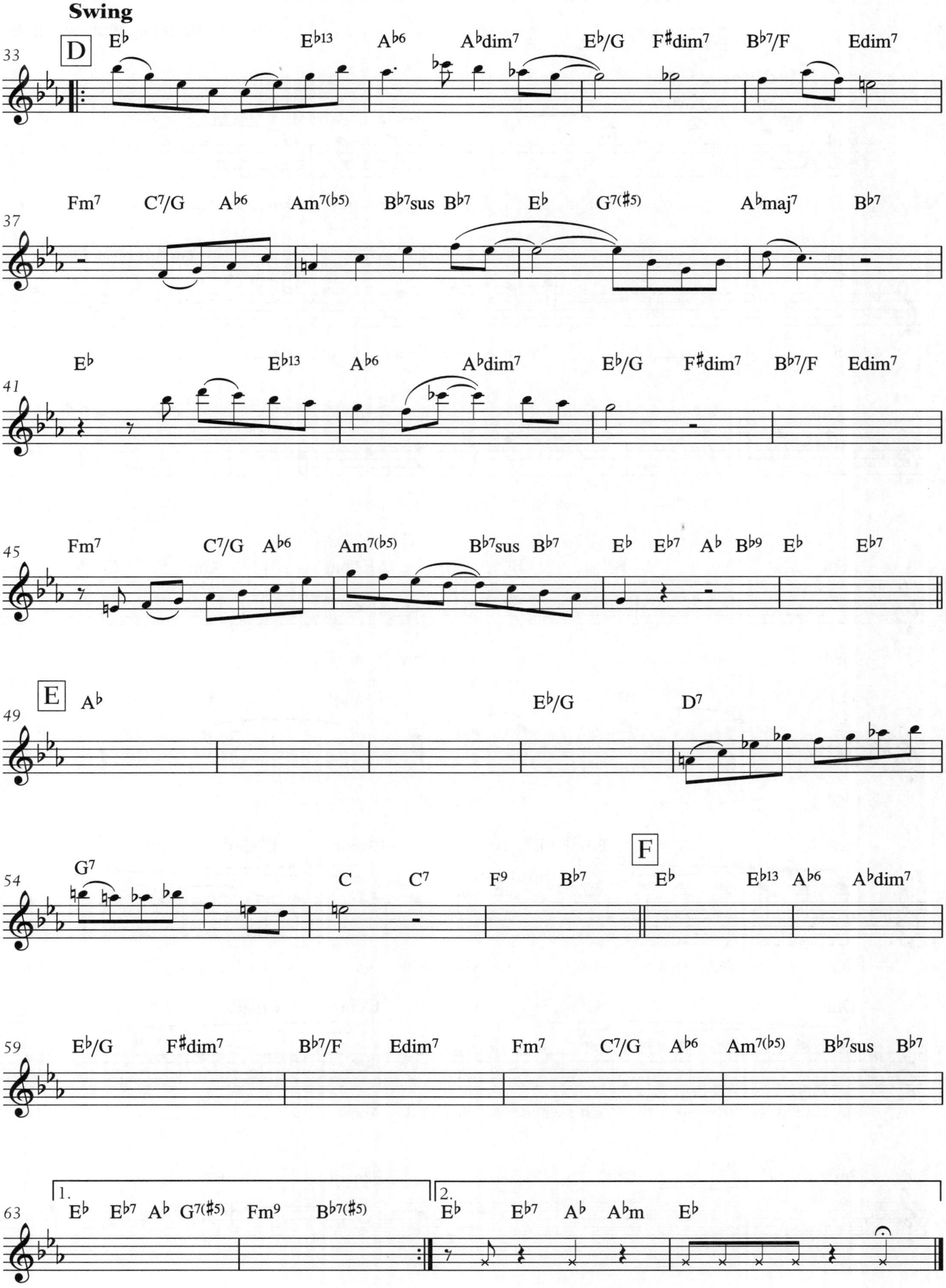

I'VE GOT YOU UNDER MY SKIN

Words and Music by Cole Porter

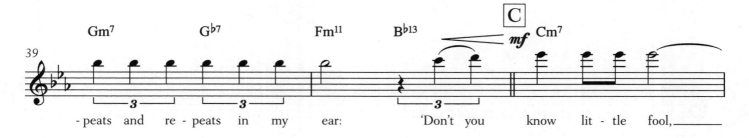

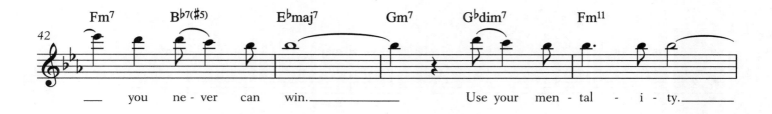

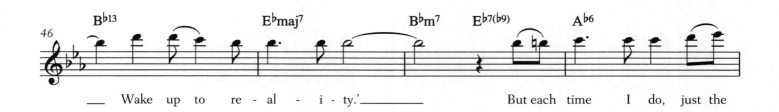

Improvisation

HOW HIGH THE MOON

Words by Nancy Hamilton
Music by Morgan Lewis

Improvisation

CD TRACK 10

I GET A KICK OUT OF YOU

Words and Music by Cole Porter

Improvisation

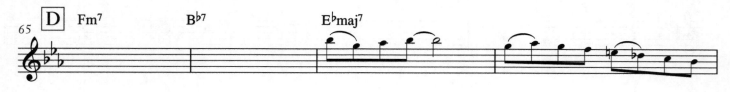

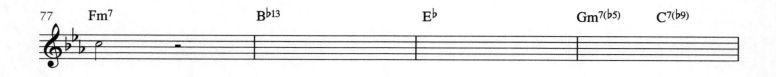

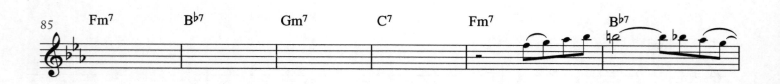

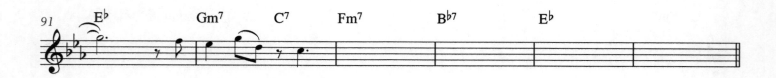

10 jazz standards and original pieces with play-along CD

JAZZ SESSIONS
FLUTE

ALEXANDER L'ESTRANGE AND TOM PILLING

FABER *ff* MUSIC

- Contains 10 standards, arrangements and original pieces with cool CD backing
- Includes 'Fly me to the moon', 'Stompin' at the Savoy' and 'C jam blues'
- Reflects a variety of jazz styles including swing, Latin, gospel and blues
- Has professional backing tracks for confident and atmospheric performance
- Includes a second, extended version of each piece for improvisation
- Ideal preparation for jazz exams, or simply for fun
- Carefully tailored for players of intermediate level (Grade 4–5)